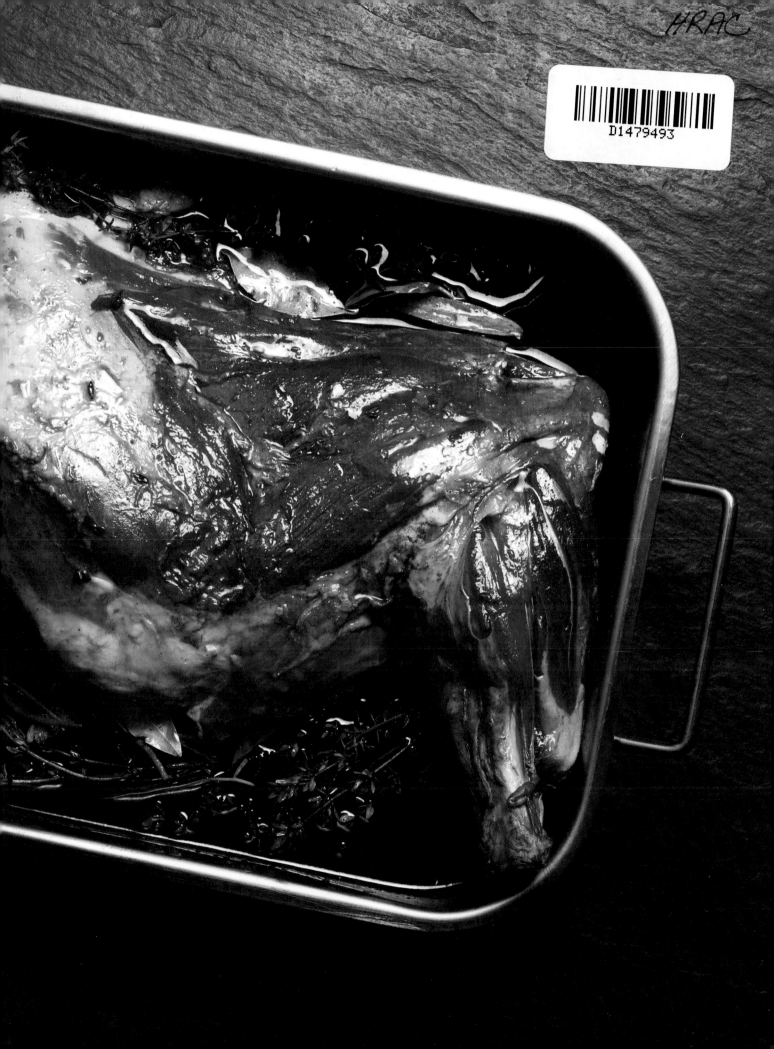

4880 Lower Valley Road • Atglen, PA • 19310

Steffen Eichhorn • Stefan Marquard • Stephan Otto

BBQ PURE

Schiffer Publishing Ltd

4880 Lower Valley Road • Atglen, PA • 19310

Other Schiffer Books on Related Subjects:

Today I Cook: A Man's Guide to the Kitchen, 978-0-7643-3644-7, $19.99
Cooking Wild Game: Thirty-six Hearty Dishes, 978-0-7643-3646-1, $19.99

Originally published as BBQ Pur! by HEEL Verlag GmbH.

Photos: Thomas Schultze, all food photos; Stephan Otto, 17, 18, 21, 28, 29; Fotolia, 19
Cover photo: Thomas Schultze
Design and Layout: Claudia Renierkens, renierkens kommunikations-design, Cologne
Food styling: Christine Birnbaum
Translated from the German by Dr. Edward Force

Type set in Eurostile/HouseMovements Soiled
ISBN: 978-0-7643-4013-0
Printed in China

Schiffer Books are available at special discounts for bulk purchases for sales promotions or premiums. Special editions, including personalized covers, corporate imprints, and excerpts can be created in large quantities for special needs. For more information contact the publisher:

Published by Schiffer Publishing Ltd.
4880 Lower Valley Road
Atglen, PA 19310
Phone: (610) 593-1777; Fax: (610) 593-2002
E-mail: Info@schifferbooks.com

For the largest selection of fine reference books on this and related subjects, please visit our website at **www.schifferbooks.com**
We are always looking for people to write books on new and related subjects. If you have an idea for a book, please contact us at proposals@schifferbooks.com

This book may be purchased from the publisher.
Include $5.00 for shipping.
Please try your bookstore first.
You may write for a free catalog.

In Europe, Schiffer books are distributed by
Bushwood Books
6 Marksbury Ave.
Kew Gardens
Surrey TW9 4JF England
Phone: 44 (0) 20 8392 8585; Fax: 44 (0) 20 8392 9876
E-mail: info@bushwoodbooks.co.uk
Website: www.bushwoodbooks.co.uk

CONTENTS

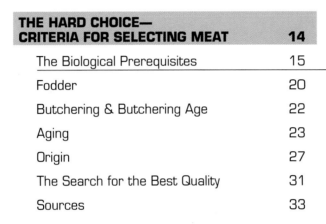

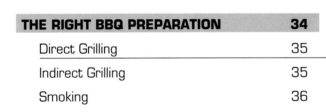

3

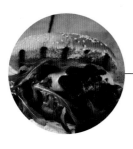

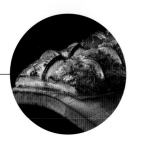

"Never change a winning team."

This well-known quotation from the legendary English soccer coach Sir Alfred Ernest Ramsey has inspired us. Our first joint project, **Pure Steak!**, has not only raised good spirits, it has been very successful. Thus the second book was assembled with the same team—for last time there was no shortage of good ideas and we were nowhere near running out of them when we reached the last page. So on to a new project!

To be sure, **BBQ Pure!** is only about barbecue; the oven definitely stays cold for these recipes. And because the quality of food is very essential for a successful BBQ experience, Stephan Otto has formulated what one must pay attention to when shopping and, above all, what one should know to put the right products on the grill. Steffen Eichhorn and Stefan Marquard are then responsible for what becomes of these carefully selected products. Recipes are worked out and then discarded, conceived anew and changed until the joy of preparation and the experience of tasting have swung to the same level. Steffen's brilliant idea of inserting colorful candies in appropriately cut melon balls and then putting them on the grill can thus be related here only as an anecdote. We laughed a lot while experimenting, but when it reached our lips, the results were—to put it mildly—rather disappointing. The recipe for grilled oysters also grew out of a very creative (experimental) phase—though with striking success. Try it yourself! We'll say no more.

But with the recipes that we have now selected, even the less experienced griller is on the right path. These recipes steer clear of pedestrian flavors and no above-average cooking experience is required to execute these dishes so that they taste the way you dreamed they would: simply delicious! Antipasti from the grill, gently cooked top round steak, eggs grilled in peppers, or New York strip in a cola and whiskey marinade—the choices are colorful, exciting, and suitable for every taste.

One last bit of advice: Where you can estimate the portions somewhat realistically, stick with it. Everybody who has smoked meat knows it doesn't pay to heat up the smoker just to feed four people. Thus in all the smoker recipes there is no prediction of how many people will presumably be stuffed full. Here too, our advice is: Try it!

And now we all wish you just as much fun as we had—and bon appetite.

Stefan Marquard

Stephan Otto

Steffen Eichhorn

THE BBQ EXPERIENCE

BBQ, or barbecue, or bar-b-que is the collective concept for the preparation, particularly of meat, over fire and flame. The necessary equipment, the grills and smokers, can be high-end toys or just a simple grill over a fire.

BBQ also stands for the culture of being together and jointly preparing meals. While one really wants to be finished in the kitchen before the guests arrive, for a **BBQ** one puts the meat on when everyone is there. The sizzling of the meat when it is put on the grill and the smoke that billows from the smoker contributes to the anticipation and pleasure of the whole experience. This event, preparing food over fire, has lasted from prehistoric times to this day, and in recent years we have been observing a **BBQ** renaissance complete with new developments and exciting innovations.

13

Besides
the right techniques
and creativity in planning and
assembling the dishes, there is a
constant in every kind of preparation.
Whether you are direct grilling for a short
period over high heat, or using indirect grilling for
a longer period over a medium temperature, or
smoking "slow and low" at a low temperature,
it is the ingredients that determine whether
the BBQ'd results are only mediocre
or remembered as an outstanding
experience.

THE HARD CHOICE: CRITERIA FOR SELECTING MEAT

The selection of quality meat involves five criteria which affect the taste, tenderness, and juiciness of your proteins: Biological prerequisites, animal fodder, butchering age, maturing, and origin and breeding. In addition, ethical criteria like the environmental awareness of the producer, how the livestock is treated throughout its lifecycle, and how transparent and easy it is to trace the product to its point of origin are also significant aspects that influence meat selection.

THE BIOLOGICAL PREREQUISITES

Whether beef, pork, or poultry—since there have been species of domesticated animals, breeders have made efforts to develop these animals further in accordance with their use.

The great majority of animal breeders in the last sixty years have become more and more oriented to the mass markets and have consequently adapted their breeding methods according to the trends of these markets. With pork in particular, this can be observed clearly, since the wishes of the industry could be put into action very quickly thanks to the very fast reproductive system. Very fast growth and fat-free meat are the requirements. The neglect of taste and ethics was knowingly taken in the bargain. The rediscovery of old German swine breeds, such as Schwaebisch Hall, or the present-day popularity of the strongly marbled half-wild black Ibérico pig shows that the gourmet cares about the same qualities that our ancestors already knew and treasured: taste, tenderness, and juiciness. Beef can be cited as a second example. Here, too, the species is very essential to the buyer. Cattle are one of the oldest breeds of domesticated animals, and there are now some 100 domestic species of cattle. Most have only regional importance, but a few are known worldwide. The breeds are classified according to their uses. Thus one differentiates between beef, milk, and dual-use species.

Breeders have tried through selective breeding to emphasize and optimize those qualities in animals which provided the highest production. The consumer in turn determined through his demand what genetics and what meat qualities continued to be bred. The first question is what motivates the consumer's choice of pork, beef, lamb, or poultry. The buyer expects certain qualities. The tenderness of the meat is particularly desired. Beyond that, a uniform quality is wanted, and as modest a price as possible. Only a few buyers expect a fair price-to-quality ratio. Proceeding from the consumers' demands, the breeders make sure that their animals are very good fodder evaluators. This means that they want to attain a high weight increase with as little fodder as possible. Their growth should also take place as quickly as possible, so the animals can be sold all the sooner. This saves not only space but also daily feeding.

For the breeder, the following criteria are also of much importance: The animals should have good maternal behavior and be robust, not susceptible to diseases. The animals' good social behavior is also important, for their peacefulness is a prerequisite for avoiding injury and it prevents their breeders from fearing their aggression.

CATTLE, SWINE, POULTRY, & MEAT PROVIDERS

Hereford, Charolais, Black Angus, Limousin, and Simmentaler, plus the Japanese Wagyu cattle, are the best-known types of **BEEF**. Wagyus, which come from the area around Kobe, Japan, are also called Kobe cattle.

The black cattle are Wagyus, the black with white heads are Wagyu-Hereford crosses, and the brown are Herefords.

Ibérico pigs

As for **SWINE**, only the old breeds have names. "Old" in this case means species that are older than seventy years. Pigs used in modern mass growing are designated as hybrids. That means they are always crossbreeds of two species that optimally unite the qualities of prolific birth, muscle size, and growth. The pig is the dominant worldwide meat provider for mankind, there are almost five times more swine butchered per year than cattle.

For the knowledgeable, critical consumer, the old breeds are more interesting; they have their reputation, are robust, can thus be raised outdoors, and stand out for higher meat quality. Popular breeds are the Schwaebisch Hall swine, also called "Moor's Head" for its black head, and the Bunte Bentheimer. In other countries the best-known species are the Bigorre, a black French pig; the Ibérico, another black pig from Spain; the Berkshire, originally from England but found today on the

menus of gourmet restaurants in the USA and Japan; and the Duroc, which has fine muscle fibers and is raised worldwide.

These old species are characterized by slower growth and more fat marbling in their meat. Thus the meat can develop flavor, juiciness, and a finer muscle fiber structure, which provides better results in the pan.

In the case of **POULTRY**, breeding has not been carried on as strongly as with the other domesticated animals. Here the various ways by which domestic and wild species are differentiated are of more interest. The domesticated animals include the chicken, duck, goose, and dove, plus the turkey. The turkey also exists as a wild bird, along with the pheasant, partridge, quail, woodcock, and Guinea fowl.

Naturally, there are well-known breeds of poultry, but these usually represent a particular region and the meat quality of that area. The best-known is the A.O.C. (Appellation d'Origine Contrôlée) Bresse poultry of southeastern France. This breed, with the French national colors (red comb, white feathers and blue feet), may be so called if it comes from the Bresse region and was raised by certain criteria. These include, among others, being fed very nutritious grain and a living space of some ten square meters per bird. It is said that the poultry in this region are treasured like aging cognac and raised like "spoiled children."

Bresse chicken

FODDER

Fodder is decisive for flavor.

The meat of animals that have been fed industrially produced mass feeds is usually tasteless. If high-priced natural fodder is used, this provides flavor. One basically differentiates between two means of feeding: Purely natural feeding, which would, for example, be grass for cattle, and feeding by a fodder program, in which further energy-rich foods are added, such as barley and corn for cattle, acorns for Ibérico pigs, or corn and cream for Mieral poultry. Though it doesn't occur often, the gourmet can find proteins that were raised on flavor-producing fodder that is part of the natural environment. Among the best examples are the Ibérico pigs which are raised in the Dehesa, the vast oak forests of southwestern Spain. This wooded pastureland provides Ibérico pigs with the nutrients they need from October through March and do not need to be fed additionally to gain flavor. The North American prairie lands, with their countless wild grasses and minerals, similarly assure the tasty, fresh flavor that the bison can develop only there.

Some types of meat, or their names, stand for the fodder that the animals have received. The best corn chickens have thus received much corn. The intensive yellow color of the corn brings about the yellowish color of the meat. American "grain-fed" beef cattle receive special fodder programs with corn and barley. The Japanese Kobe cattle are fed beer and the Ibérico pigs of "Bellota Quality" have eaten acorns.

Of course the foddering systems are basically different, but in our times it is agreed that foddering should be done with purely natural foods. The addition of hormones certainly has a positive effect — the

meat thus holds more water and is therefore potentially juicier. It is a risky undertaking, for with our present level of scientific knowledge we cannot judge for certain what the long-term effects of consuming this meat has on our overall health. The European legislators share this view, and thus the sale of hormone-treated meat has been banned in the European Union to protect the population. American lawmakers have a different view, and therefore such regulations have not been passed by Congress.

Ibérico pigs

BUTCHERING & BUTCHERING AGE

Both the tenderness and the juiciness of meat are influenced by the butchering age.

Cattle, like pigs, are full-grown at the age of 12 months. Cattle grown for the mass market are butchered at the age of 12 to 15 months. For pigs, the butchering age is between six and nine months. The cattle of the leading breeders, raised for the gourmet market, are butchered much later, at an age of 24 to 30 months. The famed Wagyu cattle are, as a rule, not butchered before 36 months. The Ibérico pigs raised by the top breeders are generally butchered between 18 and 24 months of age.

The effects of the butchering age on the quality of the meat can be explained as follows: Cattle and pigs are growing until their twelfth month. Until then the animals are not full-grown, and all their ingested energy is devoted to growth. Only when they are full-grown, after the 12th month, can their ingested energy be devoted to building up fat reserves, thus intramuscular fat. The degree of meat marbling depends very decisively on the time that is available for the animal to build up that fat. Naturally, there is also an upper limit to the butchering age. When the animals are too old, the muscle fibers become coarse and lose tenderness. This situation can be seen clearly in the bison. These wild cattle can be butchered for high-quality meat only between their 24th and 30th month.

Poultry reach their butchering age after just a few weeks. Here their names indicate how heavy—and thus how old—they were when butchered. The spring chicken, for which there is a particular demand among gourmets, is butchered earliest. As a rule, it is no more than one month old. About

four weeks later the cockerel is butchered. This can be male or female. If the chickens are butchered when two to six weeks older, they are called poulards or fattened chickens. The so-called soup chickens are the oldest. These are laying hens which are butchered after 12 to 15 months. This last group, to be sure, are not suitable for BBQ, but rather, as their name suggests, only for soup.

Since the hormones that are formed through stress have a negative effect on the meat quality, care must be taken both before and during butchering to avoid stressful situations for the animals. Thus good breeders make sure that the animals are transported only short distances before butchering or, if they must be transported farther, have enough time to settle down afterward.

The blood dove and blood duck are from France. These animals are not butchered but choked. The blood thus remains in their veins, giving the meat a more intense red color as well as more flavor. This means of killing is banned in some countries, including Germany.

AGING

There are two reasons for aging meat, especially beef.

Aging makes meat tenderer. If it ages in air—also called aging on the bone—this process has a positive effect on the flavor.

The aging process of meat can be done either in a vacuum or in air, which is done only very rarely. Aging in a vacuum is now the most commonly used method. In

the English-speaking world one differentiates between the two processes as wet aging and dry aging.

WET AGING (AGING IN A VACUUM)

When meat is aged in a vacuum, the individual pieces are vacuumed airtight after cutting and then stored and cooled precisely. The meat becomes tenderer from the release of the albumen enzyme. Today, aging is generally used only for beef. As for pork, for example, only the old breeds meet the prerequisites for aging ability. The more modern, highly bred species must be prepared right after butchering.

As one can read in studies, the aging process for beef ends after exactly four weeks at a storage temperature of 35.6°F (2°C). This means that a loss of flavor is conditionally risked if the meat is eaten before the 28th day, for it has not yet reached the maximum possible aging. Aging that lasts longer than these four weeks, though, no longer has an effect on the tenderness. Up to the point in time where the meat is no longer suitable for human consumption, the meat undergoes controlled decomposition. As a rule, the meat is given a minimum consumption date of three months by the producer, provided it is kept in its original vacuum pack and the cold chain is maintained. As soon as the meat is taken out of the vacuum, its use time is shortened, for the aging depends very strongly on the temperature and contact with air. This is especially relevant for storage in showcases in which higher temperatures prevail.

Poultry, like most pork, is usable for only a few days after butchering and needs no specific aging period to become tenderer. In France one occasionally finds meat enthusiasts who also let poultry age for several weeks, but this is not done to make the meat tenderer, but to intensify the flavor. This poultry ages in air. To make this possible, the head and feet,

as well as the edible innards, are left on the animal. Only the inedible parts are removed through a small incision. Thus the butchered animal offers only a very small area for bacteria to attack, which allows longer aging.

A further sign of quality in butchered poultry is the matter of whether the bird was plucked dry or with the use of hot water. Dry plucking is better for quality, but is more laborious. Yet it has the advantage that the meat is not contaminated as quickly as it is when it is wet.

DRY AGING (AGING IN AIR)

The traditional method of aging is aging on the bone in air. This process became known and perfected for beef in the United States. Gourmets are familiar with steak houses that age their porterhouse steaks, rib-eyes, New York strips, or T-bone steaks in their own aging chambers. Depending on where you live, it may be difficult to find aged-on-the-bone meat for barbecuing, for the disadvantages prevail among producers. For example, more refrigerator capacity has to be made available. Meat stored in a vacuum can be packed in cases and stacked. During the dry-aging process this is not possible, for air must circulate freely around the meat.

Similarly, the steak fan may not find wet-aged meat at many butcher shops—and not at all in the supermarket. For aging in a vacuum often makes the meat too expensive for the normal consumer, and the more expensive meat usually remains in the showcase.

Besides the longer, more laborious storage of dry-aging meat, the meat also loses some of its saleable weight. For one thing, the water content decreases, making the meat somewhat firmer. For another, the external tissue either dries out too much or is coated with mold—the smell in such a dry-aging chamber is very reminiscent of cheese mold—and

the dried or moldy meat has to be cut or pared off before sale and consumption. Only 50% to 70% of the original weight remains saleable, which naturally affects the sale price, and very few gourmets are ready to pay it. Thus this process is not suitable for the mass market.

But even when the price is accordingly higher, the meat lover should still try this meat, for dry-aged meat fully opens new sensory dimensions. The meat takes on an intensive flavor with a sweet taste.

THE OPTIMAL DEGREE OF AGING

When it is a matter of determining the optimal aging point, there is disagreement, for it depends on the desired intensity of flavor and juiciness or tenderness. The two effects that occur in this aging process are, first, the increase in flavor and, second, the fact that the meat loses water and thus dries out. This results in the meat being firmer when bitten the longer it ages. If the aging were extended over months and years, the results would be dry-aged bacon. This can, of course, be very tasty, but is too firm for steak on the grill, and even the smoker could no longer make it tender.

But cultural aspects also play a role in deciding on the right degree and the appropriate method of aging. The dry-aging process is much more popular in the United States, for the flavor is most important there and a firmer bite is not judged negatively. But dry aging also has an upper limit; normally the meat is aged 28 to 35 days, but there are exceptions in which the aging periods are 40, 50, or 60 days. In other markets, the tenderness of the meat is most important, thus one would rather decrease the flavor to get tenderer, juicier meat.

Dry-aged meat available on the German and European markets is normally aged 21 days. Meat that is aged longer on the bone is generally protected by being carved so that, for example, it is covered with a thick layer of fat. Thus it is sealed so that it can gain only a little flavor and not dry out.

For poultry, lamb, and veal, the animals are so young when butchered that they still have very fine fibers and thus need no aging to gain tenderness. Then, too, a very delicate flavor is wanted in lamb and veal, so that flavor intensification by aging is not desired.

ORIGIN

BEEF, PORK, & POULTRY

It is more and more important for the modern consumer to know where the foods that he/she consumes come from. This is particularly applicable to meat.

With the number of scandals about rotten or tainted meat, the existence of poor raising conditions, to which the animal-protection organizations and the Slow Food movement repeatedly call attention, this change in awareness is no surprise.

The Morgan Ranch in Nebraska

People want to know where the food, and especially the meat that they eat, come from. Our species, of course, has been nourishing itself on meat for tens of thousands of years, while large-scale animal raising and its disturbing results have become more obvious only in recent years, especially for pigs, chickens, and cattle. The consequences that influence the consumer are varied. Some react by no longer buying "denounced" meat products, whether only temporarily as a reaction to a newly revealed scandal or as a matter of principle.

Only very few consumers are lucky enough to have sources of the best-quality beef close at hand. Other than Ireland, there is no outstanding beef-producing nation in Europe that stands for very good meat quality. Growers in Germany who raise their animals with care usually have only a few animals to butcher per year, and if one does not know the grower personally, one has no chance to buy this meat.

If one looks around the world, one will always find regions in which animals are grown properly, and where it is possible, because of the plant life, to raise and butcher great numbers of them. The United States, Canada, South America, and Australia have apparently unlimited pastureland, on which cattle can be kept outdoors extensively all year. Spain, with its vast oak forests offers half-wild Ibérico pigs, and the

Ibérico pigs

Bresse of France, as already noted, provides ten square meters of land for each of its A.O.C. chickens. Thus the E.U. guidelines on required space for poultry is very clearly exceeded.

Thus it will also be a fact in the future that the meat fan, when he/she wants the best meat, will shop not regionally but globally. For this we need the dealer or butcher we trust, who can make sure that our concepts of origin and proper handling apply to the meat that we eat.

A WORD ON FISH

While man, through breeding, feeding, and deliberate determination of the butchering age and aging, has extensive influence on the quality of meat, when it comes to fish, we still depend more on nature than on human control. The best fish is caught in the wild. As for raised fish, it should be raised in as close to a wild state as possible. This type of breeding is often called permanent production.

Decisive for the quality of fish is, besides a water quality in which the fish feel good and take in no harmful materials, the water temperature. The colder the water and the more even the temperature, the more slowly and steadily the fish grow. The gourmet then receives a fish with firm meat. Besides the water conditions, naturally, the food influences the flavor of the fish. Nature, with its changing food plan, is responsible for making the fish taste good. Unlike red meat, fish is better the fresher it is, because it needs no aging. When it is properly frozen and thawed, then fish that is flash frozen on the fishing boat is the freshest that one can buy.

The size of the fish is also very decisive for the gourmet: The bigger the fish, the thicker the fillets or back pieces. This makes plating and serving easier and makes it simpler to reach the right cooking point. In top-class

gastronomy in particular, this aspect is very important, and there one pays a suitably high price for a certain quantity. In Japan, prices are charged—and also paid—for the best quality that are scarcely imaginable elsewhere. In January 2011, two Japanese gourmets auctioned a bluefin tuna with the extraordinary weight of 754 lbs (342kg) for some $406,000, representing a price of almost $540 per pound. Quite apart from the size, the bluefin tuna is on the IUCN (International Union for Conservation of Nature and Natural Resources) Red List of species under threat of extinction.

A further criterion that determines the quality is the undamaged quality of the fish. If it has indentations, such as are caused by pressure from a net, this can negatively influence its desired even consistency.

The constantly growing demand for fish from permanent growing, and the ban on catching endangered species, show our concern for an intact environment. Organizations like the Marine Stewardship Council give the consumer information to help decide what to buy.

There are no types of fish that are especially suitable for barbecuing. Basically, one can grill any fish. Yet it is important to consider the means of preparation. There are fish that are better grilled whole, while others are better prepared with their skin and still others without it. Fish with rough scales are generally eaten without skin, even though they were thoroughly scaled before preparation, for the rough skin influences the dining experience. Here the consistency of the grilled material and the right cooking point are more decisive than the kind of fish.

THE SEARCH FOR
THE BEST QUALITY

When one has done "everything right" in the purchase...

That means once you've chosen the right breed, you know that the animal was raised properly, fed properly, butchered at an optimal age, and perhaps even aged under the stated conditions, what do you do now to get the product directly onto the grill without losing any of its quality?

When buying fresh meat, the window of time for the purchase becomes smaller as far as the optimal quality is concerned. For fish, the time span is even shorter, for even if the cooling process is applied optimally, the fish's quality declines considerably after two or three days.

One thing that has changed this window in recent years are developments in the flash freezing process — the meat and fish fan has an alternative to fresh products.

This process is also called fresh frozen, meaning that products are flash frozen at the optimal maturation point for the purpose of sealing in the product's best quality. Poultry, which is very prone to fast degeneration, can thus be bought and then consumed if one has the time and peace to prepare it. For beef, the steak fan is guaranteed that he/she can eat it after an optimal aging period depending on the aging process. For Ibérico pigs, one is guaranteed that the pigs are butchered after

an optimal diet of acorns over a term of three to five months, and thus receive the "Bellota Quality" seal. Only Ibérico pigs that are butchered between January and March attain this highest level of quality.

In the past, frozen meat was principally ranked lower than fresh meat. It was not wanted on the grills of ambitious BBQ fans. This was justified, for the technique of freezing was still insufficient. If products were frozen too long, they formed large ice crystals in their tissues, which destroyed the cells, and thus a lot of fluid flowed out during thawing. Thus the meat soon became dry when roasted, and bacteria and germs could spread faster in the damaged cells.

In the flash-freezing process, the product freezes so fast that one need not fear loss of quality, since the formation of ice crystals is reduced. One must just make sure that the meat is thawed properly. This should take place slowly and at a low temperature, best done in the refrigerator. If it thaws too fast, such as at room temperature, ice crystals would form again, which would then damage the cells.

Some fish are flash frozen on the boat within a few minutes of being caught, or at the latest, the day the boat arrives in harbor, to maintain optimal freshness.

The rarer and more costly a product is, the more likely it has been fresh frozen.

SOURCES

Steak and fish fans who seek high-quality products for a BBQ can choose between two sources.

If you are planning regional or local meat for the grill, then your preparations lead you to the butcher or fish dealer you trust — someone who can, you hope, answer any questions about the above essential criteria and the quality of his/her product. In many areas it is also possible to find a direct source in a regional breeder or fisher.

For example, if you are, say, celebrity French chef Daniel Boulud, you only want the best and therefore build personal relationships directly with the fishermen you trust. If you would like to have fish, you phone the appropriate fishermen before they come into the harbor and tell them you would like to have the best fish from their catch. They can send them express to arrive the next day.

This is surely a laborious procedure that is not practicable for all. Alternatively, one can also buy from internationally recognized top-quality dealers who maintain cold chain logistics to send meat and fish to the gourmet's house. Exactly as when choosing a regional source, one must also make sure that these dealers can and will maintain the criteria responsible for the quality of the products. Naturally, quality has its price, and the principle is: The higher the quality, the higher the price. Since there are only a few consumers who can afford the best quality every day, one should consider well in advance when meat will be the exception to the weekly menu.

THE RIGHT BBQ PREPARATION

DIRECT GRILLING AT 390°F (200°C) TO 660°F (350°C)

Ground Rules

Everything that can be grilled quickly is suitable for direct grilling. Whether it is filet mignon, ribeye, roast beef, tender shoulder steaks; fillet and loin steaks of lamb or pork; or tender parts of poultry like the breast—the choice is vast. For this kind of preparation, the meat absolutely must be tender, for the grilling serves only to provide the meat with the roasting aroma and the temperature.

HOW IT'S DONE

In direct grilling, the meat is placed directly over the source of heat, either—as with a charcoal grill—directly over the glowing coals, or—as with a gas grill—directly over the burner. The danger in direct grilling is that the meat can burn or dry out very quickly. Also, using this method can create grease fires as the fat drips onto the coals or the burner.

INDIRECT GRILLING AT 320°F (160°C) TO 425°F (220°C)

In principle, one uses tender pieces for indirect grilling. The difference from direct grilling is that large pieces are used here. For example, a complete beef roast or fillet, a whole rack of lamb with bones, a lamb shoulder, whole ducks, turkeys, or quails are suitable for indirect grilling.

These pieces need a long time to bring them to their cooking point. If one grilled them only over direct heat, they would be burned on the outside before they reached the right temperature inside.

HOW IT'S DONE

For this type of grilling, the meat does not lie directly over the source of heat, but in the area near it, without heat directly under it. The most important utensil for indirect grilling is a cover. There are various kinds of indirect grilling. On a charcoal grill, the charcoal is arranged on the left and right sides and the meat is placed in the middle so that there is no direct heat below the protein. Closing the lid creates air circulation similar to that of a convection oven. For larger pieces of meet or whole birds, only one side of the grill can be supplied with charcoal, thus forming a larger surface for indirect grilling. With a gas grill, only one or two burners can be lit, and the meat can lie in the area where no burner is on.

SMOKING AT 195°F (90°C) TO 320°F (160°C)

A "slow and low" preparation is suitable for warm smoking proteins with a lot of binding tissue (also called collagen). In this cooking process, which takes hours, collagens turn into easy-to-bite gelatin. Thus lower-priced pieces, unsuitable for other types of preparation, are usually used for smoking. As a rule, cuts appropriate for smoking are from muscle groups that the animal used extensively. Whether they are necks, breasts, or shoulder pieces, the slow cooking process is suitable for making each piece tender and chewable.

The best-known pieces are the brisket (breast tip) of beef, the pork shoulder (for pulled pork), and ribs. But rack of ox, lamb neck, and poultry are also suitable.

HOW IT'S DONE

There are two types of smokers, the horizontal and vertical. The principle is the same in both types, the meat has no contact with the source of heat. It is cooked only by the constant moderate temperature and the smoke. Thus pieces of meat that would otherwise need to be cooked for hours can be prepared.

In the horizontal smoker, a small fire is made in the side box or firebox; the smoke and the warm air pass through the cooking chamber and cook the meat. In the vertical smoker, charcoal in the lower part of the grill produces the desired heat, and over it is a bowl with water, which deflects the direct heat. Over this is the meat, which is cooked gently. To attain the desired smoked flavor, one adds damp wood chips, such as beech, oak, or fruit wood.

The art of smoking consists of keeping the temperature and the smoke constant.

BEEF

BURGER DE LUXE

4 PORTIONS

INGREDIENTS		
1 ⅛ lb (500g)	Ground beef
4	Burger buns
2	Shallots, chopped
1	Orange, zest and juice
2 Tbsp (30ml)	Truffle butter (or 1 tsp (5ml) truffle oil)
½ cup (50g)	Dried tomatoes in oil
8 Tbsp (120ml)	Old balsamic vinegar
1	Truffle
4	Slices brie
	A handful of arugula

PREPARATION

Dice the shallots and sauté in the truffle butter in a pan, cut the dried tomatoes small and add them. Then add the orange zest and juice. Pour the balsamic vinegar over everything and let it reduce.

Now divide the ground beef into four equally large patties, salt and pepper them to taste, and grill directly for about 2½ minutes on each side. Cut the buns and put them on the grill for the last minute.

Spread the reduced balsamic sauce on the burger buns, cover the bun with arugula, lay the grilled patty and brie on top, and finally, dress with several truffles. Place the bun's other half on top.

And the tastiest burger in the world is finished...

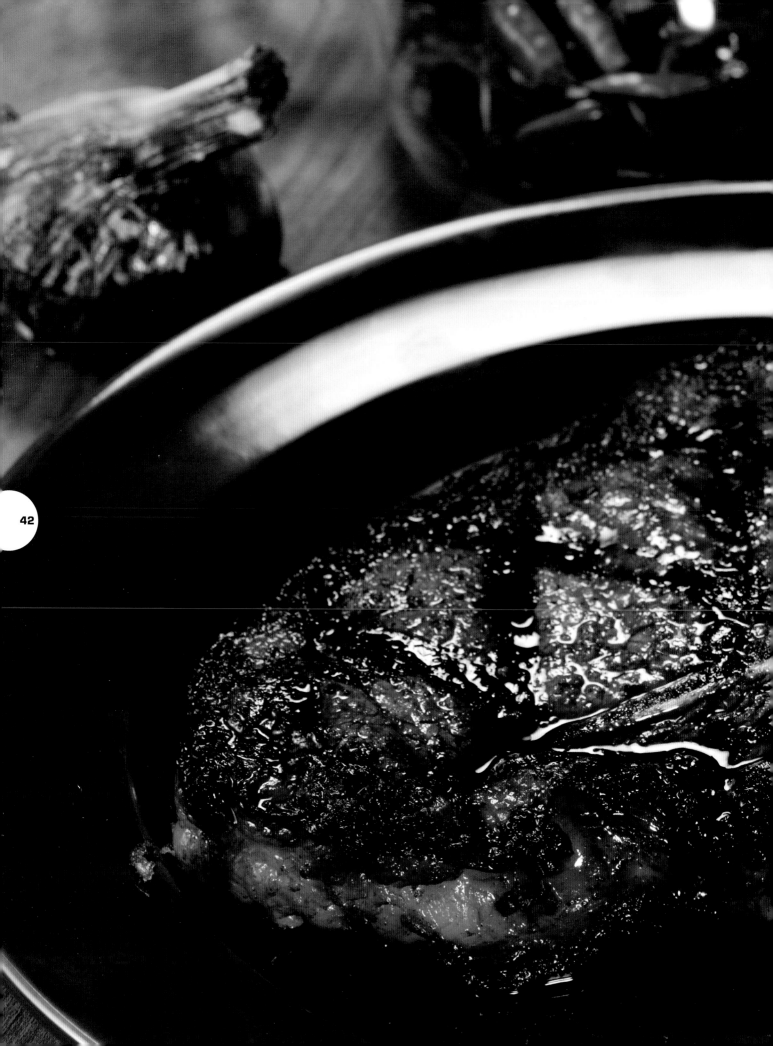

PORTERHOUSE STEAK KANSAS STYLE

4 PORTIONS

INGREDIENTS

2	Porterhouse steaks, ~1¾ lbs (800g) each
2 Tbsp (30ml)	Garlic powder
2 tsp (10ml)	Chili flakes
2 Tbsp (30ml)	Sea salt
2 Tbsp (30ml)	Black pepper
3 Tbsp (45ml)	Brown sugar
3 Tbsp (45ml)	Paprika powder
3 Tbsp (45ml)	Worcestershire sauce

PREPARATION

Mix all the ingredients—except the steaks—in a bowl. Spread it on the steaks and marinate in the refrigerator for 3 hours. Prepare the grill and grill the steaks directly for 6 minutes on each side. Sprinkle with some sea salt and let them rest briefly. Then cut the steaks into slices about ⅜ in (1cm) thick and divide among four plates.

4		New York strips ~½ lb (250g) each
5	Tbsp (75ml)	Brown sugar
3	Tbsp (45ml)	Bourbon whiskey
10	Tbsp (150ml)	Cola
3	Tbsp (45ml)	Worcestershire sauce
3	Tbsp (45ml)	Soy sauce
2	tsp (10ml)	Lemon zest
3	tsp (15ml)	Black pepper

PREPARATION

Put the ingredients—except the meat—in a bowl and mix well at room temperature. Marinate the steaks in it for at least 6 hours. After marinating, pat the meat dry and grill directly for 3 minutes on each side. Gather the rest of the marinade and heat briefly. Take the steaks from the grill and put them in a warm bowl. Pour the heated marinade over them and let stand 5 minutes before serving.

NEW YORK STRIP IN COLA WHISKEY MARINADE

4 PORTIONS

BEEF ROLLS

2¼ lb	(1kg)	Top round
1, 6-oz bag	(200g)	Leaf spinach
1⅛ lb	(500g)	Bacon slices
5 cloves		Garlic
		Olive oil
		Salt
		Pepper

Double-prong, metal skewer suitable for grilling.

For serving, stick the rolls on small wooden skewers.

PREPARATION

Cut the top round into thin, flat slices about ¾ x 1⅛ in (2 x 3cm).

Dice the garlic and remove the spinach leaves from the stem.

Put the meat in a bowl, salt and pepper them, add the garlic and some olive oil, and stir everything well.

Roll up each slice of meet with a spinach leaf and a half-slice of bacon and put on a double skewer. Depending on the skewer's size, put five to seven rolls on each skewer.

Now grill the skewers directly for one minute on each side and then cook them 5 minutes in indirect heat.

IRISH HEREFORD TENDERLOIN

4 PORTIONS

INGREDIENTS

1	Center cut beef tenderloin, 2¼ to 3⅓ lbs (1 to 1½kg)
2 Tbsp (30ml)	Fresh parsley
2 Tbsp (30ml)	Fresh basil
1 Tbsp (15ml)	Fresh thyme
1 Tbsp (15ml)	Fresh tarragon
2 Tbsp (30ml)	Fresh chives
2	Shallots
2 cloves	Garlic
¾ cup (100g)	Pine nuts
	Salt
	Pepper
2 Tbsp (30ml)	Olive oil
2 Tbsp (30ml)	Sesame oil

48

PREPARATION

Put all ingredients—except the meat—in a mixer and purée to a smooth mixture. Coat the tenderloin with this purée and put on the indirect part of the grill. Insert a thermometer into the thickest part of the meat and grill to an internal temperature of 135°F (58°C). Take the meat off the grill and rest covered for 10 minutes. Cut into slices for serving.

TIP: This dish tastes especially good when it is made with Chianina steaks, an Italian cattle breed.

50

BISTECCA FIORENTINA WITH WHITE BEANS

4 PORTIONS

INGREDIENTS

2	Porterhouse steaks, ~2¼ lbs (1kg) each
6 Tbsp (90ml)	Olive oil
4 sprigs	Rosemary
4 cloves	Garlic
2 tsp (10ml)	Black pepper, fresh-ground
2 tsp (10ml)	Sea salt
1 tsp (5ml)	Fresh oregano

SIDE DISH:

1 can	White beans in salted water
2 cans	Peeled tomatoes
3 cloves	Garlic
1 handful	Fresh sage leaves
	Salt
	Pepper
	Olive oil

White Beans:

Drain off the salt water from the beans. Heat the olive oil in a pot, sauté the garlic and sage leaves lightly. Add the tomatoes and beans and let simmer 20 minutes over low heat. Flavor with salt and pepper.

Steak:

Chop the garlic and oregano small, brush the steaks with olive oil. Mix the garlic, oregano, salt, and pepper and rub on both sides of the steaks.

Lay the rosemary sprigs on them and marinate for 12 hours. Grill the steaks 7 minutes on each side. Then let the meat set in indirect heat for 10 minutes. Cut the steaks into strips some ¾ inches (2cm) wide at right angles to the bone for serving and divide among the plates. Serve the beans separately in a small bowl.

GENTLY COOKED TOP ROUND STEAK

52

INGREDIENTS			
1			Top round steak, ~4⅓ to 6⅔ lbs (2 to 3kg)
2 cloves			Garlic, chopped
			Juice of two lemons
2 tsp	(10ml)		Curry powder
1 tsp	(5ml)		Turmeric
1 tsp	(5ml)		Coriander, ground
1 Tbsp	(15ml)		Paprika
1 tsp	(5ml)		Black pepper, fresh-ground
1 tsp	(5ml)		Salt
4 cups	(1l)		Orange juice

SMOKER

PREPARATION

Mix all ingredients well—except the meat and orange juice—and rub the steaks with it, then let marinate overnight in the refrigerator. Heat the smoker to 250°F (120°C) and hold the temperature. Smoke the beef about 4 hours to an inner temperature of 140°F (60°C). Spray repeatedly with the orange juice.

After the beef is done cooking, take the meat from the grill and let it rest 10 minutes in aluminum foil. To serve, cut against the grain.

WHOLE RACK OF OX FROM THE SMOKER

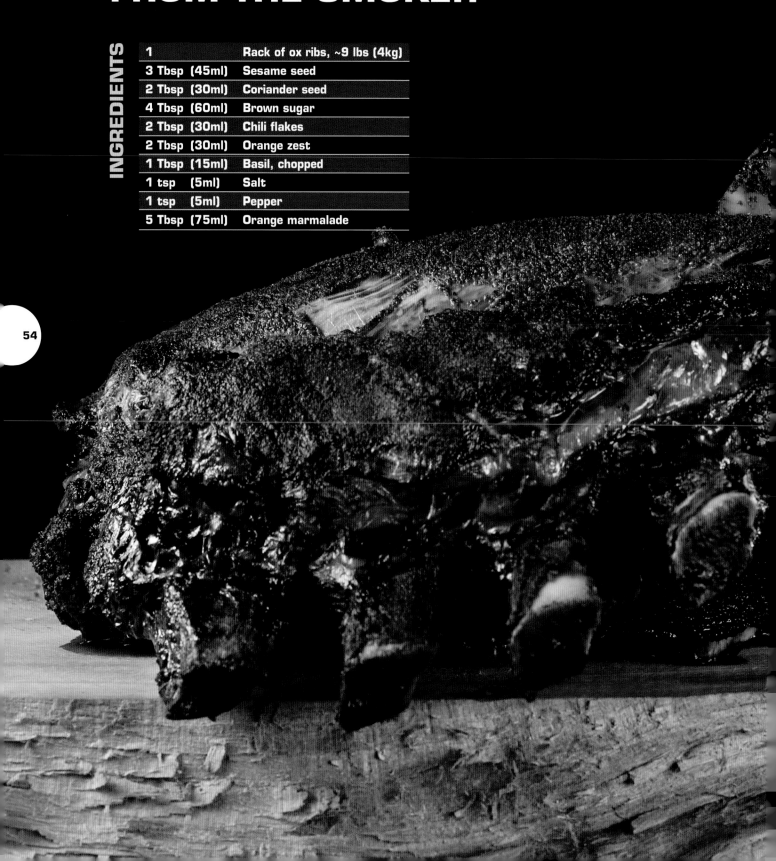

INGREDIENTS		
1		Rack of ox ribs, ~9 lbs (4kg)
3 Tbsp	(45ml)	Sesame seed
2 Tbsp	(30ml)	Coriander seed
4 Tbsp	(60ml)	Brown sugar
2 Tbsp	(30ml)	Chili flakes
2 Tbsp	(30ml)	Orange zest
1 Tbsp	(15ml)	Basil, chopped
1 tsp	(5ml)	Salt
1 tsp	(5ml)	Pepper
5 Tbsp	(75ml)	Orange marmalade

PREPARATION

Pat the ox rack dry, mix the herbs well and rub the meat with them. Coat the rubbed meat with the orange marmalade. Then heat the smoker to 230°F (110°C) and hold the temperature. Smoke the ox with apple wood, so it takes on a slight smoky flavor. Insert a thermometer into the ribs and smoke it to an inner temperature of 140°F (60°C). After cooking, take the meat from the smoker and let stand 10 minutes. Cut into slices to serve.

SMOKER

56

PREPARATION

Rub the brisket with the rub and marinate in the refrigerator for 12, or even better, 24 hours. Take it out of the refrigerator at least 3 hours before smoking so it can reach room temperature. If the meat has a temperature of only 50°F (10°C), the cooking time will be 2 hours longer! Now smoke the brisket at a low temperature between 215 and 250°F (100 and 120°C), until it reaches an inner temperature of at least 195°F (90°C). Brush the brisket for the first time with the glaze after about 5 hours, using a basting or silicone brush, and repeat this process every 30 minutes.

When the inner temperature reaches at least 195°F (90°C), take the meat from the smoker, wrap in aluminum foil, and let stand at least 20 minutes. The cooking time should range from 12 to 15 hours.

BEEF BRISKET

INGREDIENTS

1	Beef brisket, ~9 lbs (4kg)

FOR THE RUB:

5 Tbsp (75ml)	Brown sugar
5 Tbsp (75ml)	Paprika
1 Tbsp (15ml)	Ground cayenne pepper
1 Tbsp (15ml)	Garlic powder
1 Tbsp (15ml)	Onion salt
2 Tbsp (30ml)	Black pepper, fresh-ground
1 Tbsp (15ml)	Sea salt
1 Tbsp (15ml)	Ginger powder
1 Tbsp (15ml)	Ground coriander

Mix all the rub ingredients
together thoroughly.

FOR THE GLAZE:

4 cups (1l)	Apple juice (or apple cider)
1 Tbsp (15ml)	Brown sugar
1	Onion, cut into thin rings
2 Tbsp (30ml)	Paprika

Mix all ingredients together
and bring to a boil.

SMOKER

PORK

SECRETO WITH TRUFFLES

4 PORTIONS

INGREDIENTS

2¼ lbs	(1kg)	Secreto (Ibérico pork belly)
¾ cup	(200g)	Butter
1 Tbsp	(15ml)	Ground black pepper
1 tsp	(5ml)	Sea salt
1		Truffle (seasonal, black or white)

PREPARATION

Warm the butter until it melts. Take the secreto out of the refrigerator, salt and pepper it, and brush with the melted butter. Wait until the butter has solidified on the meat.

Meanwhile, prepare the grill for direct grilling at medium heat and grill the secreto 3 minutes on each side.

Then arrange the secreto on pre-warmed plates and scatter the truffles over it.

Tip: This dish is especially tasty if you use Ibérico pork.

PORK TENDERLOIN IBERIAN-STYLE

INGREDIENTS

2		Pork tenderloins
2 cloves		Garlic, chopped
1 tsp	(5ml)	Chili flakes
2 Tbsp	(30ml)	Sea salt
2 Tbsp	(30ml)	Black pepper
3		Lemons, for zest
3 Tbsp	(45ml)	Olive oil
		Some dry sherry
		Olives to serve

PREPARATION

Mix the garlic with the lemon zest, chili, sea salt, pepper, and olive oil. Coat the meat with it and marinate 4 hours in the refrigerator.

Prepare the grill for indirect grilling and grill the meat strongly on each side in the direct area, then move it to the indirect area and grill 12 minutes there until finished.

Let it stand 5 minutes, then cut the meat into slices and divide among four plates. To serve, drip a few drops of dry sherry and olive oil over it.

PORK LOIN STUFFED WITH MUSHROOMS

4 PORTIONS

INGREDIENTS

1		Pork loin in one piece, ~2¼ lbs (1kg)
16	(~60g)	Dried mushrooms
2		Spring onions
1 bunch		Parsley
4 Tbsp	(60ml)	Oil
5 Tbsp	(75ml)	Flour
3 Tbsp	(45ml)	Bacon cubes
2 oz	(50g)	Manchego cheese
		Salt
		Pepper
		Butcher's twine

PREPARATION

Soak the mushrooms in warm water for 30 minutes, then dry well.

Cut the onions, celery, and cheese finely. Mix along with the mushrooms, olive oil, bacon, and flour. Salt and pepper and let stand 30 minutes.

Cut a pocket lengthwise in the meat and fill it with the mixture. Tie with butcher's twine so the stuffing doesn't fall out.

Prepare the grill for indirect grilling, put the meat in the indirect area and grill at 390°F (200°C) for about 40 minutes.

Let it stand briefly, then cut into slices.

MALLORCAN PORK SHOULDER

4 PORTIONS

INGREDIENTS

2¼ lbs	(1kg)	Pork shoulder, boned and skinned
4 dozen		Grape snails, ready to cook
½ lb	(200g)	Chorizo
1 can		Tomatoes, skinned
5 cloves		Garlic
¼ lb	(100g)	Bacon cubes
⅜ cup	(100ml)	Olive oil
1 bunch		Parsley
1 bunch		Rosemary
1 bunch		Chives
		Marjoram
		Salt
		Pepper
		Paprika
1 dash		Red wine

PREPARATION

Flavor the pork shoulder with salt, pepper, and paprika.

Prepare the grill for indirect grilling. Grill the shoulder strongly on all sides and then put it in indirect heat. Grill indirectly at about 390°F (200°C) for an hour with the lid closed.

Meanwhile, heat the olive oil in a big pot. Cube the chorizo small, peel the garlic and chop it finely. Sauté the chorizo, bacon, snails, and garlic in the olive oil and baste with the tomatoes. Cut the herbs small and mix into the pot. Add a dash of red wine and simmer for 20 minutes. Flavor with salt and pepper.

Slice the pork shoulder thinly and serve with the sauce.

MINI BEER KEG
SUCKLING PIG

INGREDIENTS

1	Suckling pig, ~**11 lbs (5kg)**
1	5-liter mini keg of beer, any type
½ cup (60g)	Black pepper
⅓ cup (100g)	Salt
⅞ cup (100g)	Paprika, sweet
2 bulbs	Garlic
3	Eating onions
	Butcher's twine
2¼ lbs (1kg)	Pork fat

PREPARATION

Flavor the pig inside with salt, pepper, and paprika. Peel the garlic and onions, chop crudely and put inside the pig.

Sew up the abdomen at the front and back until only a hole the size of the mini keg remains open.

Use up all but about one liter of beer and remove the keg top. Now fit the pig with its abdomen over the keg and put it on the indirect part of the grill.

Heat the pork fat in a pot until liquid and brush it onto the pig repeatedly.

The cooking time is about 5 hours.

PULLED PORK SANDWICHES

1		**Pork neck, whole, ~5½ lbs (2½kg)**
RUB:		
8 Tbsp	(120ml)	Brown sugar
5 Tbsp	(75ml)	Paprika, sweet
1 Tbsp	(15ml)	Coriander, ground
2 Tbsp	(30ml)	Onion powder
1 Tbsp	(15ml)	Garlic powder
1 tsp	(5ml)	Cayenne pepper
1 Tbsp	(15ml)	Ground black pepper
2 tsp	(10ml)	Salt
1 tsp	(5ml)	Ground cumin
1 tsp	(5ml)	Chili flakes
GLAZE:		
2 Tbsp	(30ml)	Of the rub
⅜ cup	(100ml)	Vinegar
2		Onions, cut into rings
2		Habaneros
2 cups	(½l)	Beer
8		Burger buns

PREPARATION

Mix the ingredients well for the rub. Put aside 2 tablespoons of it for the glaze. Cover the pork thoroughly with the rub and refrigerate for at least 12 hours.

Put the ingredients for the glaze in a pot and boil briefly.

Heat the smoker and regulate it at 230 to 250°F (110 to 120°C).

Smoke the meat about 12 hours with little smoke from beech or fruit wood.

After 8 hours, brush with the glaze every 30 minutes.

When the pork reaches an internal temperature of 195°F (90°C), wrap it firmly in aluminum foil and let it set in a room-temperature cooler for an hour.

Pull the pork apart with two forks, and portion it out on burger buns. A green salad goes perfectly with these sandwiches.

SMOKER

RIBS FROM THE SMOKER

INGREDIENTS

4	Half-racks (7-8 ribs)

RUB:

5 Tbsp (75ml)	Brown sugar
3 Tbsp (45ml)	Paprika, medium spicy
1 Tbsp (15ml)	Salt
1 Tbsp (15ml)	Ground pepper
1 Tbsp (15ml)	Ground chili
1 Tbsp (15ml)	Onion powder
1 Tbsp (15ml)	Garlic powder
2 Tbsp (30ml)	Sesame

GLAZE:

2 cups (½l)	Orange juice
3 Tbsp (45ml)	Honey
2 Tbsp (30ml)	Of the rub
1 Tbsp (15ml)	Ground ginger
2 cloves	Garlic, whole, peeled

PREPARATION

Rub the ribs with the rub and marinate
for 12 hours.

Heat the smoker to 250°F (120°C) and hold
the temperature.

Mix the ingredients for the glaze, bring to a boil in a pot, and
reduce to a spreadable sauce.

Smoke the ribs with the meat side down for 2 hours, then turn
over and brush with the glaze.

Within the total cooking time of some 3½ to 4 hours,
brush the ribs with the glaze three times in all.

The ribs are finished when the bones
can be pulled out.

PORK

73

SMOKER

LAMB

LAMB CHOPS AFRICAN-STYLE

4 PORTIONS

INGREDIENTS		
12		Lamb chops
HERB MIXTURE:		
2 Tbsp	(30ml)	Cumin seeds
2 Tbsp	(30ml)	Coriander seeds
1 Tbsp	(15ml)	Cardamom seeds, shelled
1		Stick cinnamon
1 tsp	(5ml)	Cloves
1 Tbsp	(15ml)	Black pepper
1 Tbsp	(15ml)	Turmeric
1 Tbsp	(15ml)	Salt
MARINADE:		
1		Papaya
2		Onions
1 clove		Garlic
1 piece		Ginger, ~¾ in (2cm)
½ cup	(100g)	Greek yogurt

PREPARATION

Broil the ingredients for the herb mixture in a pan for 10 minutes and then crush them in a mortar.

For the marinade, cut all ingredients small and put in a mixer along with the herb mixture.

Mix everything well and marinate the lamb chops in it for 6 hours.

Prepare the grill for direct grilling. Pat the lamb chops dry and grill 2 minutes on each side.

Sprinkle some coarse sea salt over them and serve.

LAMB

77

LAMB LEG WITH HERB CRUST

INGREDIENTS

1	Lamb leg, ~4½ lbs (2kg)

HERB CRUST:

2 Tbsp	(30ml)	Watercress
2 Tbsp	(30ml)	Basil
2 Tbsp	(30ml)	Thyme
2 Tbsp	(30ml)	Tarragon
2 Tbsp	(30ml)	Chives
3		Shallots
5 cloves		Garlic
2 tsp	(10ml)	Horseradish, frsh.
		Salt
		Pepper
2		Day-old rolls, Torn crudely
1		Hard-boiled egg
2 Tbsp	(30ml)	Dijon mustard
8 Tbsp	(120ml)	Olive oil

PREPARATION

Put all the ingredients for the herb crust—except the olive oil—in a mixer and mix well, gradually add the olive oil until a creamy mixture results.

Take the lamb out of the refrigerator at least 2 hours before grilling and let it rise to room temperature.

Salt and pepper the lamb and brush with the herb marinade.

Prepare the grill for indirect grilling and put the lamb in the indirect area. It is best to use an internal thermometer. Grill the lamb until an inner temperature of 150°F (65°C) is reached; this takes about 2 ½ hours.

Take the meat from the grill and let it rest 5 minutes. Then cut thin slices with a sharp knife and serve.

LAMB SHOULDER PICKLED IN RED WINE

4 PORTIONS

INGREDIENTS		
1		Lamb shoulder, boned, ~2¼ lbs (1kg)
⅔ cup	(150ml)	Red wine
4 Tbsp	(60ml)	Red wine vinegar
8 Tbsp	(120ml)	Olive oil
2		Bay leaves
2		Tarragon leaves
2 sprigs		Thyme
2		Sage leaves
2		Onions
2 cloves		Garlic
		Black pepper
		Sea salt

80

PREPARATION

Peel the onions and garlic and cut into thin rings.

Wash the herbs and pat dry.

Stir the red wine, the vinegar, and 6 tablespoons of olive oil.

Put half the onions, garlic, and herbs into a bowl.

Put the lamb shoulder on them and cover with the other half.

Pour the red wine marinade over it and marinate in the refrigerator for 12 hours.

Prepare the grill for indirect grilling and put the lamb shoulder in the indirect area. Cover and cook for 2 hours.

Take the meat from the grill and let it rest 5 minutes, then slice thinly.

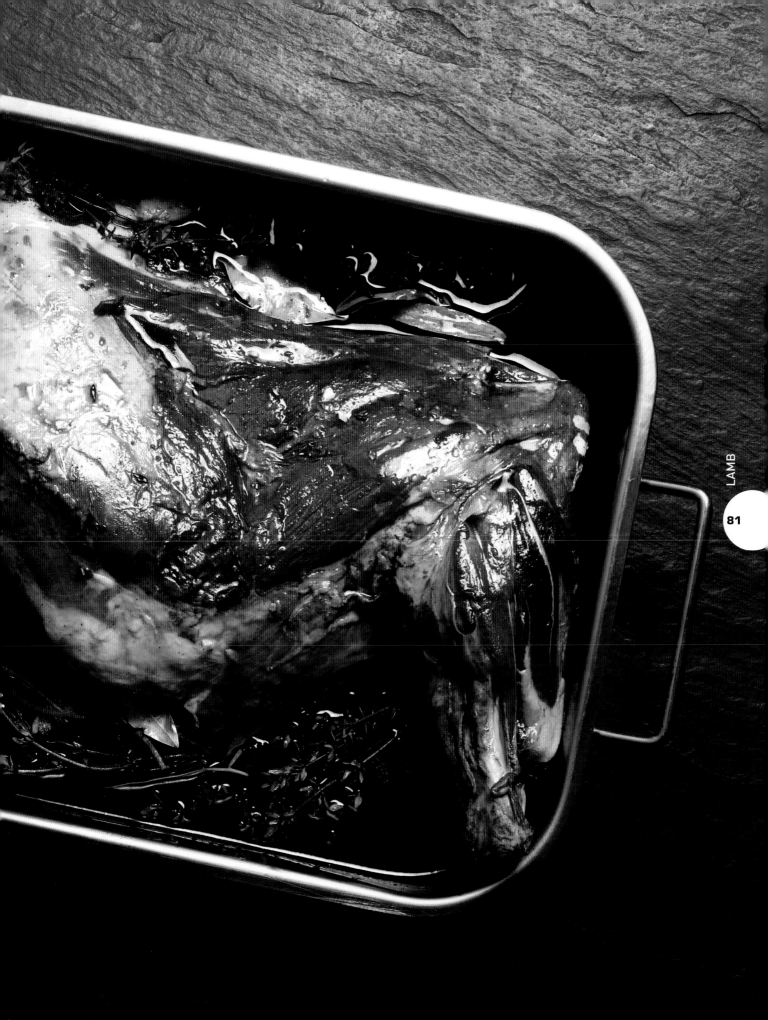

RACK OF LAMB MIAMI BEACH-STYLE

4 PORTIONS

INGREDIENTS

2	Racks of lamb
1	Ripe papaya
½ cup (100g)	Greek yogurt
1	Habanero chili pepper
	Juice of two limes
1	Red onion
1 clove	Garlic
	Salt
1 pinch	Sugar
	One more papaya
	Lemon juice

PREPARATION

Peel the papaya and cube small, remove the seeds from the habanero and cut it small, peel the onion and garlic and cut small. Put them all in a mixer with the yogurt, salt, lime juice, and sugar and mix well.

Brush the lamb with the marinade and marinate in the refrigerator for 12 hours.

Prepare the grill for indirect grilling. Take the meat out of the marinade and pat dry. Grill the lamb directly for 2 minutes on each side, then put in the indirect area and grill 10 minutes at about 390°F (200°C) until finished.

After grilling, let the lamb rest for 5 minutes and then cut individual cutlets.

Peel the second papaya and cube small, drip lemon juice on it. Plate the cutlets and serve with the papaya.

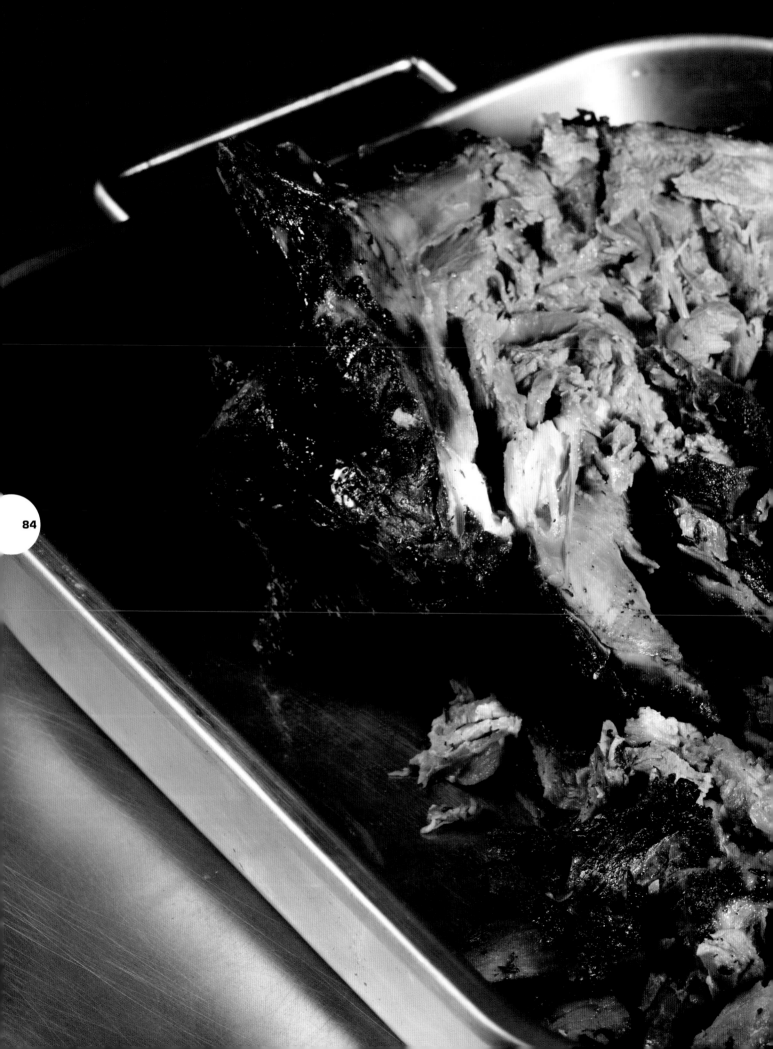

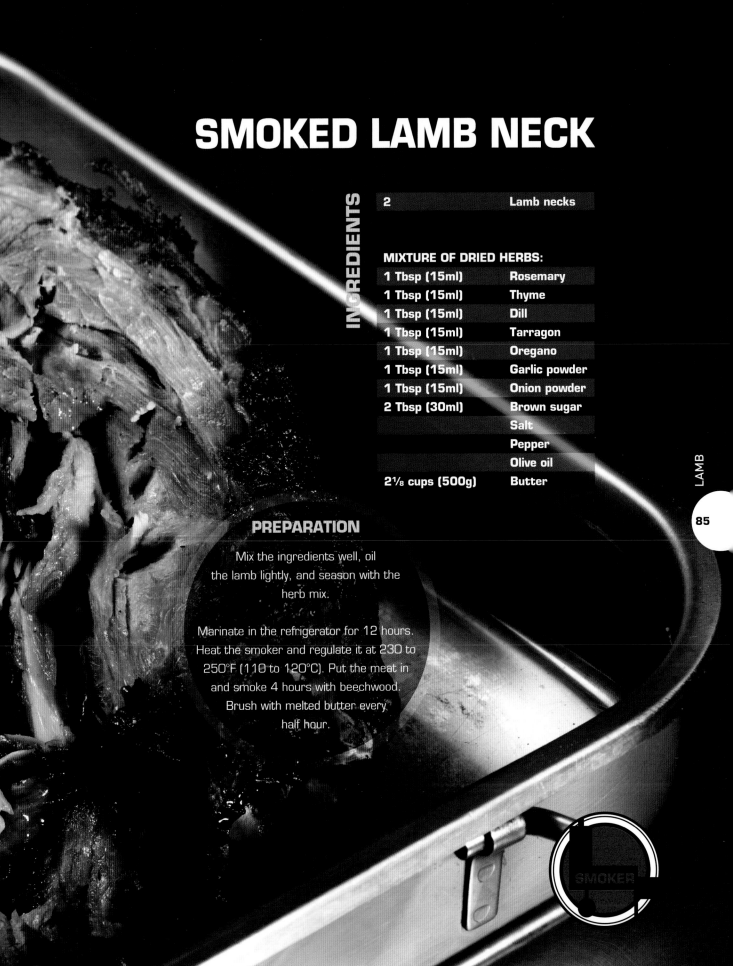

SMOKED LAMB NECK

INGREDIENTS

2	Lamb necks

MIXTURE OF DRIED HERBS:

1 Tbsp (15ml)	Rosemary
1 Tbsp (15ml)	Thyme
1 Tbsp (15ml)	Dill
1 Tbsp (15ml)	Tarragon
1 Tbsp (15ml)	Oregano
1 Tbsp (15ml)	Garlic powder
1 Tbsp (15ml)	Onion powder
2 Tbsp (30ml)	Brown sugar
	Salt
	Pepper
	Olive oil
2⅛ cups (500g)	Butter

PREPARATION

Mix the ingredients well, oil the lamb lightly, and season with the herb mix.

Marinate in the refrigerator for 12 hours. Heat the smoker and regulate it at 230 to 250°F (110 to 120°C). Put the meat in and smoke 4 hours with beechwood. Brush with melted butter every half hour.

SMOKER

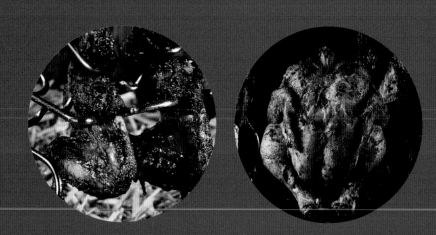

POULTRY

HOT SMOKED CHICKEN WINGS

INGREDIENTS

2¼ lbs (1kg)	Chicken wings
1 Tbsp (15ml)	Paprika
2 Tbsp (30ml)	Garlic, granulated
4 Tbsp (60ml)	Brown sugar
2 Tbsp (30ml)	Salt
2 Tbsp (30ml)	Coriander, crushed
1 Tbsp (15ml)	Mustard powder
2 Tbsp (30ml)	Cayenne pepper
1 Tbsp (15ml)	Cumin, ground
2 Tbsp (30ml)	Black pepper, ground
1 Tbsp (15ml)	Chili flakes
2 cups (500ml)	Sweet chili sauce

PREPARATION

Wash the chicken wings thoroughly under
running water and pat dry. Mix the spices and rub
on the chicken wings.

Heat the smoker to 230°F (110°C) and
hold the temperature.

Put the chicken wings in the smoker and smoke 3 ½ hours
with little smoke.

After 2 hours, brush them with the chili sauce,
and repeat this every 20 minutes.

WINGED TRILOGY

INGREDIENTS

1	Quail
1	Chicken
1	Duck
1 can	Red Bull®
1 can	Cola
1, 1l can	Beer

FOR THE BRINE:		
12 cups	(3l)	Cola
4 cups	(1l)	Orange juice
5 Tbsp	(75ml)	Ground pepper
8 Tbsp	(120ml)	Sea salt
4 Tbsp	(60ml)	Chili powder
4 Tbsp	(60ml)	Paprika
4		Red onions
5 Tbsp		Thyme
1		Ginger root, cut small (~1⅛ in [3 cm])
8 Tbsp	(120ml)	White wine or cider vinegar
10 Tbsp	(150ml)	Brown sugar

PREPARATION

1.
Put the three birds in the brine in a watertight container overnight and cover. Take them out the next morning, pat dry, and refrigerate 3 hours. Then oil them slightly, salt and pepper well, and coat liberally with the rub.

2.
Fill the three cans ⅓ with white wine.

3a.
Set the quail on the Red Bull can...

3b.
...the chicken on the cola can and...

FOR THE RUB:

10 Tbsp (150ml)	Lime zest
	Salt
	Pepper
2 bunches	Thyme
6 Tbsp (90ml)	Paprika
	Olive oil
2 cups (500ml)	White wine

3c.
...the duck on the beer can.

4.
Prepare the grill for indirect grilling. First put the duck on the indirect area of the grill, the chicken about an hour later, and the quail 15 minutes after that.

Grill temperature: 390°F (200°C)

Cooking times:
Duck: 2 hours
Chicken: 1 hour
Quail: 45 minutes

FISH & SHELLFISH

93

MELON & HALIBUT SKEWERS

4 PORTIONS

INGREDIENTS

2	Halibut fillets
1	Honeydew melon
4 Tbsp (60ml)	Honey
4 Tbsp (60ml)	Horseradish, grated
	Salt
	Pepper
4	Skewers

PREPARATION

Debone the halibut fillets and remove the skin.

Cut each halibut fillet into 16 equally sized blocks, salt and pepper them.

Peel the melon and cut 16 equally sized blocks, roughly the size of the fish.

Alternate fish and melon blocks on the skewers. Mix the horseradish with the honey and brush on the skewered blocks. Let them set for an hour.

Prepare the grill for indirect grilling. Grill the skewers directly briefly on each side and then leave in the indirect heat for 7 minutes.

BEECH PLANK SALMON

INGREDIENTS

1	Salmon, skin on, ~3⅓ lbs (1½kg)
1	Beech plank, untreated, ~¾ in (2cm) thick, soaked in water at least 1 hour

FOR THE MARINADE:

2 Tbsp (30ml)	Lime juice
2 Tbsp (30ml)	White vinegar (apple, wine, or rice)
2 Tbsp (30ml)	Dijon mustard
2 Tbsp (30ml)	Honey
2 Tbsp (30ml)	Chives, chopped
1 tsp (5ml)	Salt
½ tsp (2½ml)	Garlic, granulated
½ tsp (2½ml)	Black pepper
¼ tsp (1¼ml)	Cayenne pepper
4 Tbsp (60ml)	Olive oil

PREPARATION

Mix the ingredients for the
marinade thoroughly in a mixer. Mix in
the oil gradually to form a smooth mixture.

Now salt and pepper the salmon. Score the
skin—do not cut all the way through the skin—and
brush lavishly with the marinade.

Then lay the salmon on the board with the
skin-side down and grill directly for 20
to 25 minutes at 355 to 390°F
(180 to 200°C).

PIERCED PERCH

3 PORTIONS

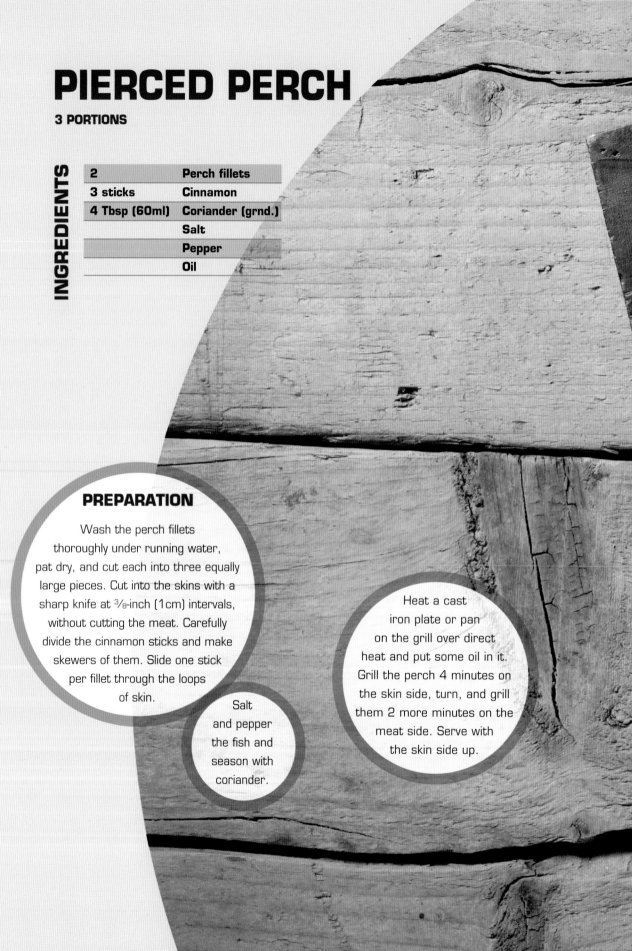

INGREDIENTS

2	Perch fillets
3 sticks	Cinnamon
4 Tbsp (60ml)	Coriander (grnd.)
	Salt
	Pepper
	Oil

PREPARATION

Wash the perch fillets thoroughly under running water, pat dry, and cut each into three equally large pieces. Cut into the skins with a sharp knife at ⅜-inch (1cm) intervals, without cutting the meat. Carefully divide the cinnamon sticks and make skewers of them. Slide one stick per fillet through the loops of skin.

Salt and pepper the fish and season with coriander.

Heat a cast iron plate or pan on the grill over direct heat and put some oil in it. Grill the perch 4 minutes on the skin side, turn, and grill them 2 more minutes on the meat side. Serve with the skin side up.

SALMON TROUT

PREPARATION

Wash the trout thoroughly under running water. Wash the potatoes and cut about ⅜ inch (1cm) straight off the bottoms. Cut through the fish skin with a sharp knife at 1⅛-inch (3cm) intervals, making sure that the meat is not cut. Then rub the fish with the lemon juice and let it stand for 30 minutes.

Cut the thyme, parsley, chives, and garlic small. Put the chives and half the herbs aside. Mix the rest with the lemon zest, salt, pepper, and olive oil and rub the fish thoroughly with it.

Prepare the grill for indirect grilling at medium heat. Stick the potatoes into the abdominal opening of the fish with their flat sides down and put the fish in the indirect heat, standing on the potatoes.

Melt the butter and mix the chives and other herbs into it.

Grill the fish 30 to 35 minutes and brush with butter every 10 minutes.

GRILLED OYSTERS

4 PORTIONS

102

INGREDIENTS		
12	Oysters
½ cup (125g)	Butter
½ bunch	Parsley, chopped
½ bunch	Chives, cut into small cylinders
2	Small red chili peppers, such as bird's eye
2	Lemons for juice and zest
1 clove	Garlic, chopped finely
1 Tbsp (15ml)	Salt
1 Tbsp (15ml)	Black pepper
3 Tbsp (45ml)	Brown sugar

PREPARATION

Mix all the ingredients, except the oysters and lemon juice, thoroughly with the butter. It is best to put the butter in a preheated oven first. Now shuck the oysters, pour off the water, sprinkle with lemon juice, and cover each with a teaspoon of the herbs and butter. Grill the oysters directly for 10 minutes.

SIDES

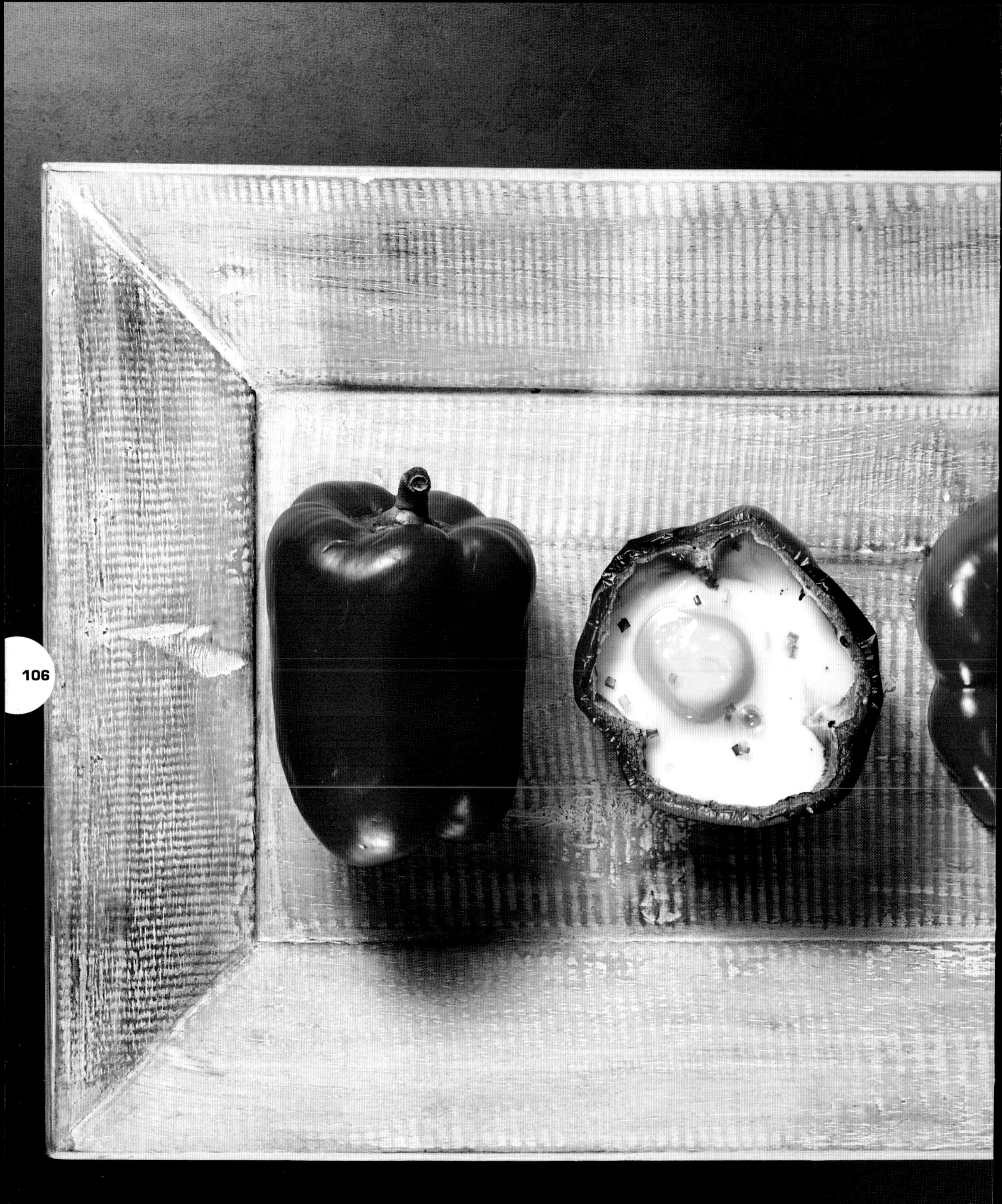

EGGS GRILLED IN RED PEPPERS

4 PORTIONS

INGREDIENTS

4	Red peppers
4	Eggs
	Salt
	Pepper
	Paprika
	Chili flakes
2 Tbsp (30ml)	Chives, diced

PREPARATION

Cut off about one-third of the pepper, directly below the stem. Remove the seeds and inner membranes.

Season the peppers inside with chili flakes, open each egg and put it in a pepper. Now salt and pepper the eggs and season with paprika.

Prepare the grill for indirect grilling and grill the peppers indirectly for 10 minutes at about 390°F (200°C). Remove peppers carefully from the grill with tongs, plate, and garnish with chives.

ANTIPASTI FROM THE GRILL

3 PORTIONS

INGREDIENTS

1		Muffin pan	2 Tbsp	(30ml)	Thyme, chopped small
3		Prawns	1 handful		Rose leaves, unsprayed
3		Scallops without shells	2		Lemons
3		Grape snails without shells	2 Tbsp	(30ml)	Chili flakes
¼ lb	(100g)	Beef tenderloin cut into 3 equally sized cubes	1 tsp	(5ml)	Paprika, strong
			4 tsp	(20ml)	Salt
1¾ cup	(400g)	Butter at room temperature	4 tsp	(20ml)	Pepper
6 cloves		Garlic, chopped small	Some		Sugar
2 Tbsp	(30ml)	Rosemary, chopped small			

PREPARATION

Rose butter for the scallops:
Thoroughly mix about ½ cup (100g) butter, rose leaves (rinsed in cold water and chopped small), one teaspoon salt, one teaspoon pepper, one garlic clove chopped small, and one pinch of sugar.

Put one scallop in each muffin form. Divide the rose butter over the scallops in the three muffin forms. They should be about ⅔ full.

Lemon butter for the prawns:
Thoroughly mix about ½ cup (100g) butter, zest from two lemons, one teaspoon lemon juice, one teaspoon salt, one teaspoon pepper, one garlic clove chopped small, and a pinch of sugar.

Put one prawn in each muffin form. Divide the lemon butter over the prawns in the three muffin forms. They should be about ⅔ full.

Herb garlic butter for the snails:
Thoroughly mix about ½ cup (100g) butter, rosemary, thyme, three chopped garlic cloves, one teaspoon salt, one teaspoon pepper, and a pinch of sugar.

Put one snail in each muffin form. Divide the herb garlic butter over the snails in the three muffin forms. They should be about ⅔ full.

Chili butter for the beef tenderloin:
Thoroughly mix about ½ cup (100g) butter, two tablespoons chili flakes, one teaspoon salt, one teaspoon pepper, one garlic clove chopped small, one teaspoon paprika, and a pinch of sugar.

Put one beef cube in each muffin form. Divide the chili butter over the three muffin forms. They should be about ⅔ filled.

Prepare the grill for indirect grilling, put the muffin pan in indirect heat, and grill until the butter melts.

Take the pan from the grill and put it on a heat-resistant surface. Serve with crusty bread.

TOMATOES STUFFED WITH NORTH SEA CRABS

4 PORTIONS

INGREDIENTS		
4		Large fresh tomatoes
¼ lb	(100g)	North Sea crabs, shelled
⅞ cup	(200g)	Cream cheese
1 bunch		Ramps (substitute with chives or garlic)
		Salt
		Pepper
		Sugar
		Lime juice

PREPARATION

Cut the tomato tops off ⅜ inch (1cm) below the stem and remove the pulp.

Do not dig them out too deeply, so that a bottom remains. Then cut the tomatoes flat on the bottom so they can stand up easily.

Cut the ramps small and mix with cream cheese, salt, pepper, sugar, and some lime juice. Then fold in the crab meat and fill the tomatoes with the mixture.

Grill the tomatoes in indirect heat for 20 minutes at 390°F (200°C).

STUFFED CHAMPIGNON MUSHROOMS

4 PORTIONS

INGREDIENTS		
4	Giant mushrooms
2 slices	Serrano ham, finely cut
4 Tbsp (60ml)	Grated cheese (i.e. Manchego or Swiss)
2 Tbsp (30ml)	Crème Fraîche
1	Red onion, diced into fine cubes
	Salt
	Pepper

PREPARATION

Brush the mushrooms and twist out the stems. Carefully hollow out the caps a bit with a scoop or teaspoon.

Chop the removed mushroom meat finely and mix well with the ham, onion, 3 tablespoons cheese, and crème fraîche. Season the mixture with salt and pepper and fill the mushroom caps.

Scatter the rest of the cheese on top and grill about 10 minutes under medium, indirect heat until the mushrooms are soft and the cheese thoroughly melts.

GRILLED LEEKS

4 PORTIONS

INGREDIENTS

4 stalks	Leek
4 Tbsp (60ml)	Honey
1	Ginger root (¾ in [2cm]), diced
	Sea salt

PREPARATION

Trim the dark green ends of the leeks, wash the leeks thoroughly, and carefully pull out the three or four inner rings. Cut these rings lengthwise and take out the inner rings. Now brush the trimmed leeks with honey and stuff the leek with some of the chopped ginger. Grill directly for 10 minutes, remove the outer rings before serving and cut the leek into rings about ¾ inch (2cm) wide. Sprinkle with sea salt.

STUFFED BREAD

4 SMALL LOAVES

INGREDIENTS

FOR THE BREAD:

5 cups	(500g)	Flour
1 cup	(250ml)	Water
1 tsp	(5ml)	Salt
1 pack		Dry Yeast
1 pinch		Sugar

FOR THE FILLING:

1		Zucchini
1		Eggplant
2		Tomatoes
5⅓ oz	(150g)	Feta
1 clove		Garlic, chopped
		Salt
		Pepper
		Rosemary, dried

PREPARATION

Divide the dough into four equally large parts and roll each one out round. Cut the zucchini, eggplant, tomatoes and feta in slices. Cover one half of the dough rounds with a stack of the cut-up vegetables and feta. Salt, pepper, drip on some olive oil, sprinkle on some chopped garlic, and season with rosemary. Now fold the uncovered half of the dough over the covered half and press it down about ⅜ inch (1cm) from the edge, so the bread stays firmly closed when baked. Trim off the outer edge of the dough.

Grill 15 to 20 minutes at 390°F (200°C) on a pizza slab in indirect heat.

FOR PORK

RUB:	
5 Tbsp (75ml)	Brown sugar
3 Tbsp (45ml)	Paprika, medium strong
1 Tbsp (15ml)	Salt
1 Tbsp (15ml)	Ground pepper
1 Tbsp (15ml)	Ground chili
1 Tbsp (15ml)	Onion powder
1 Tbsp (15ml)	Garlic powder

Mix all the ingredients thoroughly.

GLAZE:	
2 cups (½l)	Orange juice
3 Tbsp (45ml)	Honey
2 Tbsp (30ml)	Of the rub
1 Tbsp (15ml)	Ground ginger
2 cloves	Garlic, whole, without peel

RUBS, GLAZES, & SAUCES

FOR BEEF

RUB:	
5 Tbsp (75ml)	Brown sugar
5 Tbsp (75ml)	Paprika
1 Tbsp (15ml)	Ground cayenne pepper
1 Tbsp (15ml)	Garlic powder
1 Tbsp (15ml)	Onion salt
2 Tbsp (30ml)	Ground black pepper
1 Tbsp (15ml)	Sea salt
1 Tbsp (15ml)	Ground ginger
1 Tbsp (15ml)	Ground coriander

Mix all the ingredients thoroughly.

GLAZE:	
4 cups (1l)	Apple juice (or apple cider)
2 Tbsp (30ml)	Brown sugar
1	Onion, cut in thin rings
2 Tbsp (30ml)	Paprika

Put everything in a pot and bring to a boil briefly.

BARBECUE SAUCE

2 cans	Tomato puree
2	Medium onions, chopped
8 Tbsp (120ml)	Worcestershire sauce
½ cup (100g)	Butter
4 Tbsp (60ml)	Oil
2 Tbsp (30ml)	Sugar
2 Tbsp (30ml)	Brown sugar
2 Tbsp (30ml)	Coffee beans, fresh-ground
1 tsp (5ml)	Salt
1 tsp (5ml)	Garlic, chopped very fine
1 tsp (5ml)	Black pepper
½ tsp (2½ml)	Ground ginger
½ tsp (2½ml)	Ground pimento

Mix all ingredients, bring to a boil and let
cook for 10 minutes, stirring occasionally.

HERB FISH MARINADE

1 Tbsp (15ml)	Thyme
1 Tbsp (15ml)	Oregano
1 Tbsp (15ml)	Marjoram
1 tsp (5ml)	Ground green peppercorns
2 Tbsp (30ml)	Herb mustard
1 Tbsp (15ml)	Herb vinegar
1 Tbsp (15ml)	Parsley

Combine all the ingredients
and mix in a mixer until it is a
smooth mixture. This marinade
is suitable for all white fish such
as cod, flounder, perch, etc.

MARINADE FOR PORK, CHICKEN, & BEEF

1 ½ Tbsp (20g)		Ginger, fresh-grated
2		Chili peppers, such as bird's eye
½ tsp	(2½ml)	Cardamom
1 tsp	(5ml)	Black pepper
⅜ cup	(100ml)	Orange juice, fresh-squeezed
1 tsp	(5ml)	Soy sauce
⅜ cup	(100ml)	Olive oil

Mix everything thoroughly, rub it on the
meat and marinate for 3 hours.

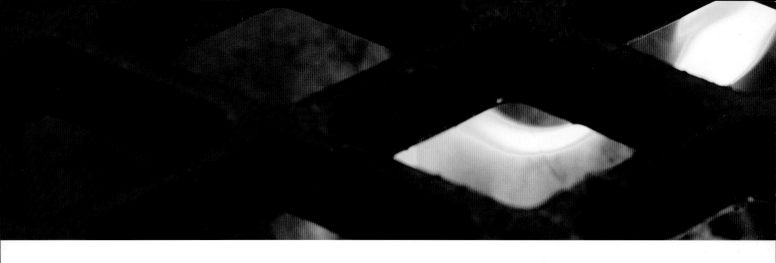

INDEX

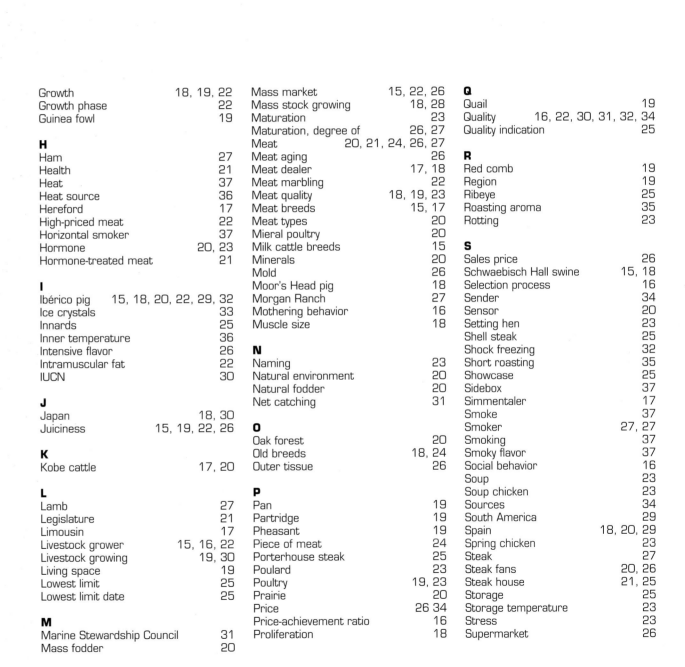

122

To prepare the following recipes, you need a smoker:

RECIPE INDEX

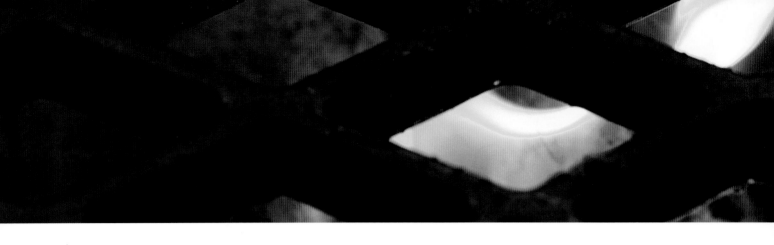

STEPHAN OTTO

At the end of 2004, Stephan Otto, born in 1966, made his hobby his profession and opened the OTTO GOURMET firm with his two brothers Wolfgang and Michael. Trained as a banker and businessman, after long years as a business advisor, he went to the United States in 2001 and worked as a management advisor. At that time he became acquainted with American beef—especially the Wagyu-Kobe style sold by mail order—which moved him to give up his profession and enter the food business, exporting this fine beef to Germany.

OTTO GOURMET is very successful in finding and marketing exclusive, high-quality meat. Stephan Otto is dedicated to the strategy and commercial development of OTTO GOURMET, and thus has an important influence on the firm's products and customer service. It is his passion and inspiration to attract lovers of good meat. The durability of production, devoted breeders, proper animal treatment, and knowing the value of top-class gastronomy—those are the important criteria by which he chooses his products.

Stephan Otto is privately a griller. He says, "Roasting aromas from the grill, along with juicy, tasty meat, makes life worth living."

STEFAN MARQUARD

Stefan Marquard, star cook, is known for his creative, somewhat different cooking style. In the kitchen he likes to listen to punk rock music and sets the standard: "What tastes good is allowed—even if it sounds laughable at first."

Born in Franconia in 1964, he was trained as a butcher and then as a cook at the Hotel Rebstock in Wuerzburg. Jobs in renowned hotels followed as he spent a year on a culinary trip through Italy. Along with Adalbert Schmid, he opened the Taverna la Vigna, which very quickly became the best Italian restaurant in the German-speaking area. In 1991 he opened his first solo restaurant, the Drei Stuben in Meersburg.

With his unconventional style, he earned, among others, a Michelin star and 18 points in the Gault Millau. From 2000 to 2003 Marquard was the chief cook in Germany's greatest restaurant, the Lenbach in Munich. Since 2003 he has run Stefan Marquards Event Catering with Wolfgang Weigler. Along with his team, the Jolly Roger Cooking Gang, he has bewitched all of Europe with his cooking skill, always true to the motto "cooking is like punk rock!" In 2010 Stefan Marquard opened two new restaurants, the Dining Range in the Olching Golf Club near Munich and a restaurant in the Bavarian Yacht Club of Munich at Starnberg.

STEFFEN EICHHORN

Born in 1976 in Franconia, Steffen pursues his passion for cooking and first-class food. When, by chance, he became aware of the Grill Sport Club website, he had found himself. His grilled dishes became increasingly more elaborate, and finally he joined the master grill team of the Grill Sport Club, winning a master's title in 2009.

For some time Steffen Eichhorn has not only worked closely with the OTTO GOURMET firm but also made his mark in barbecuing with renowned top-rank chefs like Kolja Kleeberg, Stefan Marquard, Peter Scharff, and Ralf Jakumeit. In 2009 he founded the BBQ & More firm, which offers event catering, grilling seminars, and dealer training for well-known grill manufacturers.

Pure Steak.

Steffen Eichhorn, Stefan Marquard, and Stephan Otto. Star cook Stefan Marquard, meat expert Stephan Otto, and German grillmaster Steffen Eichhorn present 39 extraordinary steak recipes. From exciting twists like Ribeye Stirred and Not Shaken and Sirloin Meets Scallop to traditional offerings like Garlic Steak and Filet Mignon, this soulful cookbook is ideal for all meat lovers.

Size: 8 1/2" x 11" • 84 color images • 136 pp.
ISBN: 978-0-7643-3927-1 • hard cover • $29.99

Cooking Wild Game: Thirty-Six Hearty Dishes.

G. Poggenpohl. Impress your guests with dishes from this classic collection of 36 European game dishes. Mouthwatering flavors and cooking styles combine with a variety of venison, wild boar, hare, duck, pheasant, and more. Accompanied by color photos, each recipe offers ingredients and cooking instructions. Prepare these hearty dishes for your next dinner party.

Size: 8 1/2" x 11" • 36 color photos • 80 pp.
ISBN: 978-0-7643-3646-1 • hard cover • $19.99

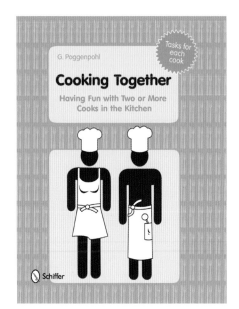

Cooking Together: Having Fun with Two or More Cooks in the Kitchen.

G. Poggenpohl. Everyone pitches in with this cookbook designed for multiple cooks in the kitchen. More than 30 recipes have two sets of instructions: for each cook or team of cooks. There's a game, puzzle, or riddle with each recipe to guarantee a fun time in the kitchen for all.

Size: 8 1/2" x 11" • 36 color photos • 80 pp.
ISBN: 978-0-7643-3647-8 • hard cover • $19.99

Today I Cook: A Man's Guide to the Kitchen.

Felix Weber. More than 40 dishes for today's man to master. Carefully-tested instructions break the preparation into easy-to-digest steps, including tips for ensuring things go smoothly. Classic dishes and impressive meals for your culinary repertoire.

Size: 8 1/2" x 11" • 61 color photos • 80 pp.
ISBN: 978-0-7643-3644-7 • hard cover • $19.99

Schiffer books may be ordered from your local bookstore, or they may be ordered directly from the publisher by writing to:

Schiffer Publishing, Ltd.
4880 Lower Valley Rd.
Atglen, PA 19310
(610) 593-1777; Fax (610) 593-2002
E-mail: Info@schifferbooks.com

Please visit our web site catalog at *www.schifferbooks.com* or write for a free catalog. Please include $5.00 for shipping and handling for the first two books and $2.00 for each additional book. Full-price orders over $150 are shipped free in the U.S.

Printed in China